WITHDRAWN

COUNTRY PROFILES

RUSSIA

BY AMY RECHNER

BLASTOFF!
DISCOVERY

BELLWETHER MEDIA • MINNEAPOLIS, MN

Blastoff! Discovery launches a new mission: reading to learn. Filled with facts and features, each book offers you an exciting new world to explore!

This edition first published in 2018 by Bellwether Media, Inc.

No part of this publication may be reproduced in whole or in part without written permission of the publisher.
For information regarding permission, write to Bellwether Media, Inc., Attention: Permissions Department, 5357 Penn Avenue South, Minneapolis, MN 55419.

Library of Congress Cataloging-in-Publication Data

Names: Rechner, Amy, author.
Title: Russia / by Amy Rechner.
Description: Minneapolis, MN : Bellwether Media, Inc., [2018] | Series: Blastoff! Discovery: Country Profiles | Includes bibliographical references and index. | Audience: Grades 3-8. | Audience: Ages 7-13.
Identifiers: LCCN 2017000866 (print) | LCCN 2017001135 (ebook) | ISBN 9781626176867 (hardcover : alk. paper) | ISBN 9781681034164 (ebook)
Subjects: LCSH: Russia (Federation)–Juvenile literature.
Classification: LCC DK510.23 .R43 2018 (print) | LCC DK510.23 (ebook) | DDC 947–dc23
LC record available at https://lccn.loc.gov/2017000866

Editor: Christina Leaf   Designer: Brittany McIntosh

Printed in the United States of America, North Mankato, MN.

TABLE OF CONTENTS

A NORTHERN LIGHT

WINTER PALACE
ST. PETERSBURG

NEVA RIVER

A family visits St. Petersburg, Russia, in June. The long hours of daylight give them lots of time to explore the city on the Neva River. The **tourists** walk through beautiful palaces, museums, and public squares. Boat tours glide down the river and canals that wind through the city.

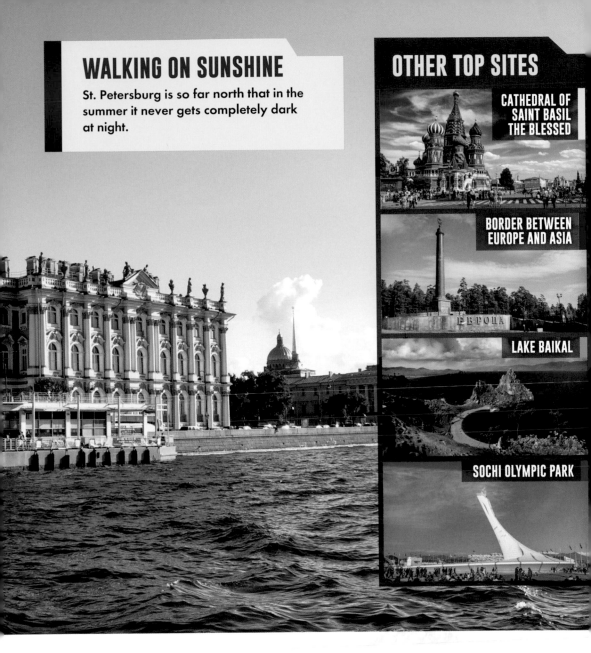

OTHER TOP SITES

CATHEDRAL OF SAINT BASIL THE BLESSED

BORDER BETWEEN EUROPE AND ASIA

LAKE BAIKAL

SOCHI OLYMPIC PARK

A favorite stop is the Hermitage Museum, Russia's largest museum. It is inside the elegant Winter Palace. St. Petersburg's unusual beauty, history, and culture are like no place else. This is Russia!

ARCTIC OCEAN

NORWAY

FINLAND

SLAVIC COUNTRIES

ST. PETERSBURG

MOSCOW

URAL MOUNTAINS

YEKATERINBURG

NOVOSIBIRSK

KAZAKHSTAN

GEORGIA

AZERBAIJAN

Russia is the largest country in the world. It stretches from Europe all the way to Asia's Pacific coast. It is nearly twice the size of the United States, with more than 6.6 million square miles (17 million square kilometers).

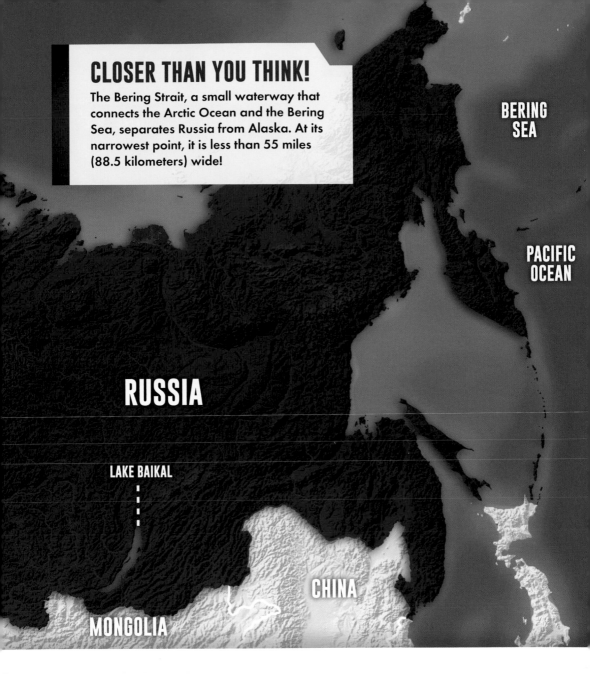

CLOSER THAN YOU THINK!

The Bering Strait, a small waterway that connects the Arctic Ocean and the Bering Sea, separates Russia from Alaska. At its narrowest point, it is less than 55 miles (88.5 kilometers) wide!

BERING SEA

PACIFIC OCEAN

RUSSIA

LAKE BAIKAL

CHINA

MONGOLIA

The capital city of Moscow is in western Russia. Norway, Finland, and several **Slavic** countries line the western border. Kazakhstan, Mongolia, and China are south. The Pacific Ocean and Bering Sea lie to the east. To the north is the Arctic Ocean.

7

LANDSCAPE AND CLIMATE

The Ural Mountains split Russia between Europe and Asia. Most of European Russia is flat **plains**. East of the mountains is Siberia. Its huge, flat plains are called **steppes**. Just north of the steppes grow enormous pine forests called **taiga**. Northern Siberia is **tundra**. Lake Baikal, the world's deepest lake, is in southern Siberia. Russia's Volga River is Europe's longest river. The longer Lena River winds through Asian Russia.

= TUNDRA   = STEPPE   = TAIGA

N
W + E
S

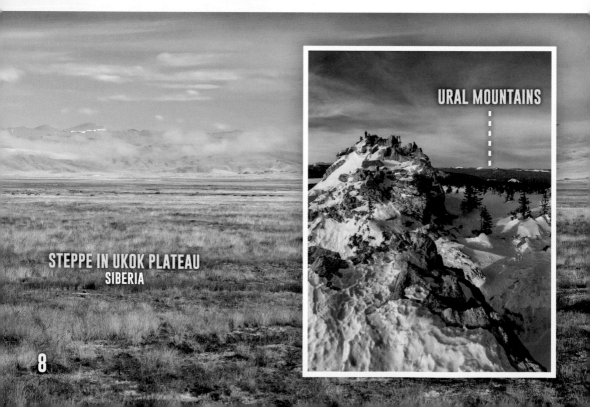

STEPPE IN UKOK PLATEAU
SIBERIA

URAL MOUNTAINS

TAIGA
EASTERN SAYAN
MOUNTAINS, SIBERIA

MOSCOW

Average
monthly highs
and lows

JANUARY
HIGH: 21 °F (-6 °C)
LOW: 14 °F (-10 °C)

APRIL
HIGH: 50 °F (10 °C)
LOW: 36 °F (2 °C)

JULY
HIGH: 73 °F (23 °C)
LOW: 57 °F (14 °C)

OCTOBER
HIGH: 46 °F (8 °C)
LOW: 37 °F (3 °C)

°F = degrees Fahrenheit
°C = degrees Celsius

Russian winters are very long and cold. Spring and fall only last a few weeks. Summers are short, but they can get very hot. It is more **temperate** in the south.

WILDLIFE

Russia's vast size and varied climate attracts many different and unusual animals. Siberian tigers and brown bears hunt prey in the taiga. The frozen tundra is home to polar bears, Arctic foxes, and musk oxen. Snow leopards lurk in the southeastern mountains.

The waters around Russia are home to gray seals, orcas, and sharks. Otters and gray herons share **habitats** near freshwater. Lakes and rivers are filled with sturgeon and trout. Owls and eagles swoop overhead in search of prey. Skylarks and nightingales fill Russia's skies with song.

MUSK OX

ARCTIC FOXES

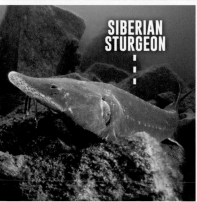
SIBERIAN STURGEON

SIBERIAN TIGER

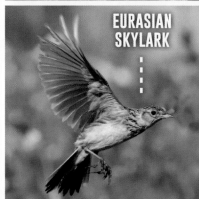
EURASIAN SKYLARK

BROWN BEAR

BROWN BEAR

Life Span: **25 years**
Red List Status: **least concern**

brown bear range = ■

LEAST CONCERN	NEAR THREATENED	VULNERABLE	ENDANGERED	CRITICALLY ENDANGERED	EXTINCT IN THE WILD	EXTINCT

More than 142 million people live in Russia. The majority of the population lives in the European part of the country. Russian Orthodox is the most common religion, but some practice other forms of Christianity or Islam. More than half of all Russians do not follow any religion.

Most people are of Russian **heritage**. Some are also from smaller **ethnic** groups that became part of Russia over time. Russian is the national language, but these groups still speak their own languages, too. Russian is written with an alphabet called Cyrillic.

FAMOUS FACE

Name: Alex Ovechkin
Birthday: September 17, 1985
Hometown: Moscow, Russia
Famous for: A professional hockey player and the captain of the Washington Capitals of the National Hockey League (NHL)

SPEAK RUSSIAN

Russian uses the Cyrillic alphabet. However, Russian words can be written with the English alphabet so you can read them.

ENGLISH	RUSSIAN	HOW TO SAY IT
hello	privet	preev-YET
goodbye	do svidaniya	doh svee-DON-ya
please	pozhalvista	pah-ZHAL-oo-stah
thank you	spasiba	spah-SEE-bah
yes	da	dah
no	nyet	nyet

MOSCOW

NIZHNY NOVGOROD

Most Russians live in small city apartments. Many generations of the same family may share one apartment. Families are small, with only one or two children. Both parents generally work outside the home. In the country, farmers may form communities on collective farms. They share the responsibility of farming the land.

Few people own cars in large cities like St. Petersburg or Moscow. They get around with public transportation or on foot. The easiest way to travel between cities is by train, although it is not always quick. Traveling across Russia could take a week!

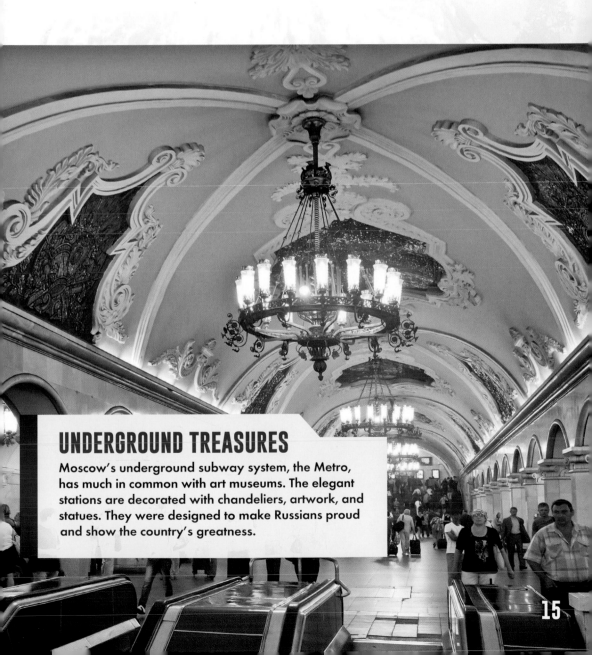

UNDERGROUND TREASURES

Moscow's underground subway system, the Metro, has much in common with art museums. The elegant stations are decorated with chandeliers, artwork, and statues. They were designed to make Russians proud and show the country's greatness.

DRESS FOR SUCCESS

Wherever Russians go, they are dressed correctly for the occasion. Russian people dress well and avoid looking too sloppy or casual. Appearance is very important!

The **communist** beliefs of the **Soviet Union** taught Russians to be good neighbors. Multiple families lived in **communal** apartments, which required people to get along and act respectfully. They used timetables to make sure everyone got equal time to use the shared kitchen or bathroom.

Even in tight quarters, friends are welcome. Hosts bring out slippers for guests to wear in the home. Tea and sweets are served. Visitors often bring small gifts. Russians enjoy talking and arguing with friends whether at home, in cafes, or in Russian sauna baths called **banyas**.

BANYA

Russian children start school early, in preschool or kindergarten. They must remain in school until age 17. After nine years of general education, students can choose to continue general education or start more specialized schooling. From there, many go to college.

Modern Russia is a very industrial country. Fewer than one in ten Russians work on farms. They grow crops like wheat or sugar beets, or they tend livestock. Mining and oil production use Russia's many **natural resources**, including iron ore and coal. Factories make goods such as machinery, cars, and clothing. Most people work in **service jobs** in areas like education or public safety.

POLICE OFFICERS

CAR FACTORY

ICE HOCKEY

Russia's professional athletes are among the best in the world. Ice hockey and basketball are just two of the team sports in which they excel. Graceful Russian gymnasts and ice skaters compete for Olympic gold. Chess is a popular game for those who prefer mental gymnastics. Russian chess players are some of the world's top players.

CHESS

Russian people also enjoy soccer and spending time outdoors hiking and camping. In the winter, ice skating and skiing are popular. The lakes and seas offer plenty of chances for swimming and fishing in summer. **Urban** families retreat to summer houses called **dachas** to enjoy nature and relax.

ENJOY THE SHOW!

Music, dance, and theater are very important aspects of Russian culture. People often spend their free time at shows and concerts of all kinds, like the world-famous Russian ballet.

REZINOCHKI

Rezinochki requires at least three players and a piece of elastic 9 to 12 feet (2.7 to 3.7 meters) long. An alternative would be a Chinese jump rope, available in some toy stores.

How to Play:

1. Knot the ends of the elastic together to make a long loop. Have two players stand inside the loop with it around both ankles. Back away from each other to stretch it. Stand with feet shoulder-width apart so the loop is a rectangle between the two players.

2. Call out a sequence of jumps that the jumper must do. If they jump the pattern correctly, they can be challenged with a harder pattern at ankle level, or the same pattern at knee level, then thigh, waist, and chest.

3. If a player misses the pattern or lands on the elastic incorrectly, they are "out." The next player tries the same pattern or is given a new one.

PINK SOUP!

Borscht is a famous Russian soup. It is known for being bright pink because it is made with beets. It is enjoyed both hot and cold.

Russian food relies on grains, dairy, and winter vegetables like beets, cabbage, and potatoes. Fish is also common. Ripe vegetables are usually pickled or dried for later use.

Breakfast is often *kasha*, a porridge made from buckwheat. The midday meal includes soup such as *borscht*, and a meat dish like beef stroganoff. The evening meal starts with an appetizer like *pirozhki*, small buns stuffed with mushrooms or meat. A hot main dish and tea follow. Dark rye bread, which is called black bread, is served at every meal.

KASHA

PIROZHKI

KISSEL RECIPE

Kissel is an easy fruit recipe that can be a drink or a Jell-O-like dessert. It can be made with any kind of fresh or frozen berries or preserves.

Ingredients:
- 12 ounces fruit jam, any flavor (with no whole fruit in it)
- 8 cups water
- 3-5 tablespoons potato starch or tapioca
- 1/4 cup cold water

Steps:
1. With adult help, whisk fruit jam with water in a saucepan on the stove until it is smooth. Bring to a boil, stirring occasionally.
2. While it is cooking, stir potato starch or tapioca in cold water until it dissolves. The more you use, the thicker the kissel will be.
3. When the jam reaches a boil, slowly add the starch liquid, stirring constantly. Keep stirring until it thickens. Then turn off the stove and let it sit while it cools for a few minutes. Kissel can be served hot or cold. If it is a Jell-O-like dessert, spoon into bowls and let it cool.

CELEBRATIONS

Russia's holiday calendar begins with New Year's. It is the biggest event of the year and includes many elements often associated with Christmas. There are trees, gifts, and a Russian version of Santa named Ded Moroz. The Russian Orthodox Christmas comes after New Year's Day. In February comes Russia's oldest holiday, *Maslenitsa*. Russians drive away the winter blues with games and *blini* pancakes. They also burn a straw doll representing winter.

Russia Day, on June 12, is the country's national holiday. Large public celebrations honor the history and accomplishments of the Russian people. Like Russia itself, it is both serious and joyful.

RUSSIA DAY

24

NEW YEAR'S
MANEZHNAYA SQUARE
MOSCOW

1237
Mongols begin their conquest of Rus, making it part of their empire

862
Eastern Slavic tribes unite under a single leader and become known as the Rus

1762
Catherine the Great becomes empress after she overthrows her husband

1547
Ivan the Terrible (Ivan IV) becomes the first czar and grand prince of all Russia

1480
Ivan the Great (Ivan III) unites Russia and pushes the Mongols out

1696
Peter the Great becomes czar and tries to make Russia more European

1928
Joseph Stalin takes full control of the Soviet Union

2014
Sochi, Russia, hosts the Winter Olympics

1917
Bolshevik rebels led by Vladmir Lenin overthrow Czar Nicholas II and take over the government, beginning communist rule

1991
Under President Mikhail Gorbachev, the Soviet Union and communism end, making Russia a capitalist society

1922
Communist leaders form the Soviet Union, a collection of conquered nations known as the Union of Soviet Socialist Republics (USSR)

2000
Vladimir Putin is elected president

RUSSIA FACTS

Official Name: Russian Federation

Flag of Russia: The flag of three equal horizontal stripes of white, blue, and red was created by Peter the Great in 1699. It went out of use at the start of communist rule in 1917, but it was re-adopted in 1991 when communism ended.

Area: 6,601,668 square miles
(17,098,242 square kilometers)

Capital City: Moscow

Important Cities: St. Petersburg, Novosibirsk, Yekaterinburg

Population:
142,355,415 (July 2016)

WHERE
PEOPLE LIVE

COUNTRYSIDE
26%

CITY
74%

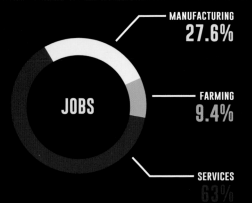

MANUFACTURING
27.6%

JOBS

FARMING
9.4%

SERVICES
63%

Main Exports:

petroleum

natural gas

wood products

metals

machinery

National Holiday:
Russia Day (June 12)

Main Language:
Russian

Form of Government:
semi-presidential federation

Title for Country Leaders:
president, premier

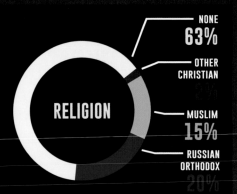

NONE
63%

OTHER CHRISTIAN

RELIGION

MUSLIM
15%

RUSSIAN ORTHODOX
20%

Unit of Money:
Ruble

GLOSSARY

banyas—public spas where people meet and sit in hot steam rooms or hot, dry saunas

communal—shared or used in common by members of a group or community

communist—related to communism; communism is a social system in which property and goods are controlled by the government.

dachas—country houses or cottages used for vacations

ethnic—related to a group of people who share customs and an identity

habitats—lands with certain types of plants, animals, and weather

heritage—the background or history of a group of people

natural resources—materials in the earth that are taken out and used to make products or fuel

plains—large areas of flat land

service jobs—jobs that perform tasks for people or businesses

Slavic—related to a group of people from Eastern Europe called the Slavs

Soviet Union—short for the Union of Soviet Socialist Republics; the Soviet Union is a former country in Eastern Europe and western Asia made up of 15 republics or states that broke up in 1991.

steppes—dry, flat land in areas with wide temperature ranges

taiga—a northern forest of trees that produce cones, like spruce and fir

temperate—associated with a mild climate that does not have extreme heat or cold

tourists—people who travel to visit another place

tundra—frozen, treeless land; beneath the surface, tundra is permafrost, or land that is permanently frozen.

urban—related to cities and city life

TO LEARN MORE

AT THE LIBRARY

Alberti, Theresa Jarosz. *Russia*. North Mankato, Minn.: The Child's World, 2015.

Ganeri, Anita. *Russia*. Chicago, Ill.: Heinemann Raintree, 2015.

Torchinsky, Oleg, Angela Black, and Debbie Nevins. *Russia*. New York, N.Y.: Cavendish Square Publishing, 2016.

ON THE WEB

Learning more about Russia is as easy as 1, 2, 3.

1. Go to www.factsurfer.com.

2. Enter "Russia" into the search box.

3. Click the "Surf" button and you will see a list of related web sites.

With factsurfer.com, finding more information is just a click away.

INDEX

The images in this book are reproduced through the courtesy of: Igor Sobolev, front cover; Juan Martinez, front cover (flag), pp. 5 (middle top, bottom), 17, 23 (top upper), 27, 28 (flag); Alan Bauman, pp. 4-5, 5 (middle bottom), 14, 18, 22 (inset), 23 (top lower); Viacheslav Lopatin, p. 5 (top); Brittany McIntosh, pp. 6-7; Alexander Demayanov, p. 8; Suhanova Kseniya, p. 8 (inset); Nikitin Victor, p. 9; Pavel Burchenko, p. 9 (inset); Vadim Petrakov, pp. 10-11; Bildagentur Zoonar GmbH, p. 10 (top); Fufachew Ivan Andreevich, p. 10 (middle bottom); Karel Bartik, p. 10 (middle bottom); Dzmitry Yakubovich, p. 10 (bottom); Aleksei Verhovski, p. 10 (bottom corner); Sergey Smolentsev, p. 12; Patrick Smith/ Staff/ Getty Images, p. 13 (top); Anton Gvozdikov, p. 13 (bottom); Raga Jose Fuste/ GLOW Images, p. 15; RosaIreneBetancourt 6/ Alamy Stock Photo, pp. 16-17; Free Wind 2014, p. 19 (top); Andrei Kholmov, p. 19 (bottom); Pukhov K, p. 20 (top); Natalia Volkova, p. 20 (bottom); Pavel L Photo and Video, p. 21 (top); Iakov Filimonov, p. 21 (bottom); HurricaneHank, p. 22; Julia Shmayaeva, p. 23 (bottom); Associated Press, p. 24; Chamille White, pp. 24-25; Oleg Mit, p. 29 (currency).